James Joseph Moriarty

Wayside Pencillings

With Glimpses of Sacred Shrines

James Joseph Moriarty

Wayside Pencillings
With Glimpses of Sacred Shrines

ISBN/EAN: 9783337331276

Printed in Europe, USA, Canada, Australia, Japan

Cover: Foto ©Thomas Meinert / pixelio.de

More available books at **www.hansebooks.com**

WAYSIDE PENCILLINGS,

WITH

Glimpses of Sacred Shrines,

BY THE

Rev. JAMES J. MORIARTY, A.M.,

CHATHAM VILLAGE, N. Y.

ALBANY, N. Y.:
VAN BENTHUYSEN PRINTING HOUSE.
1875.

PENCILLINGS BY THE WAYSIDE.

A TRIP TO EUROPE

THE contemplation of a voyage across the Atlantic is always suggestive of anxious thoughts, and sometimes of gloomy forebodings. There is always the terrible spectre of sea-sickness presenting itself to the uninitiated—to all, in fact, who are accustomed to feel the due sense of their own weight on *terra firma*. It would not be at all advisable for any one who is in the habit of walking about majestically upon the earth, who seems to be always impressed with feelings of his own superiority, and who, to make use of a common expression, always stands on his dignity, to venture on a sea voyage; for there is scarcely anything so humiliating to such individuals, so trying to their patience, so repugnant to their tastes, so opposed to their sense of dignity, and so utterly at variance with highly starched collars and unruffled linens, as the extremely annoying and disagreeable complaint familiarly called seasickness. At the same time, to see such an individual, as I have described, suffering under such untoward circumstances is not unfrequently, I know not by what perversity of human nature, relished by the best of men. As to the unhappy mortal whose system has to undergo such a fearful purification as is necessary for a healthy renovation, you may divide his sea voyage into three periods. In the first part of the trip he feels, and wishes to convince his fellow-passengers of the same, that he is certainly going to die, that there is no hope that he can possibly survive such a terrible attack, such a fearful upheaving of nature. A more pitiable object, a more forlorn, hopeless, dilapidated-looking being you can only find on sea. He would certainly be willing to pay three times the fare to be once more on land, and be sure of his foothold on the earth (if not of his standing in the community), than ever to wander again far away from the comforts of home.

I remarked that in the first part of his voyage the unhappy sufferer is constantly afraid he is going to die; but, alas, in the second part of his trip, he is sadly lamenting that death did not come to his rescue. His sufferings he considers unbearable, and he consequently sinks into a sad and gloomy despondency, sorrowfully resigned to inexorable fate. In the third and last period, however, a faint hope begins to gleam on him that perhaps he may survive; the fearful phantoms begin to disappear; unpleasant reminiscences of a stomach at sea are expelled from the mind; the pale, emaciated, but now hopeful patient, humbly yet stealthily takes his allotted place at his first morning meal, and then begins to look about for the beauties of nature. It is wonderful, then, how quickly his sentiments and habits change, how warmly he praises the invigorating sea-breeze, and dilates most enthusiastically on the glorious beauties of sunrise on the ocean; and he retires to his couch meditating on the calm serenity of the atmosphere and the glories of the firmament. When he happily reaches the land he plants his foot soldier-like on mother earth, as much as to say, none but women and children fear the sea!

LA BELLE FRANCE.

Arriving in France towards the end of May, one is surprised to find vegetation so far advanced, and a long voyage on sea renders the scenery all the more charming. After leaving Havre, a large, well-built seaport, *en route* for Paris, you are immediately impressed with the truthfulness of the name given to the country—*La Belle France*—for it is, indeed, most beautiful, with its smiling, verdant fields, its charming villages, its quaint old towns, its curiously tiled houses, its venerable abbeys and cathedrals. The country through which I passed was not only lovely on account of the ever-varying scenery, but also for its wonderful fertility and many evidences of prosperity.

In passing through the venerable city of Rouen, a glance would sufficiently indicate its rank and importance, situated, as it is, on the right bank of the Seine, and affording a fine harbor for a great number of vessels. In this famous old city, formerly the capital of Normandy, that most heroic Christian maiden, JEANNE D' ARC, was cruelly burned to death by the English, who were then in possession, on the 30th of May, A.D. 1431, just four hundred and forty-three years to the very day that I gazed on the old gabled houses of that remarkable city. So it is not in Ireland alone that we find traces of English tyranny and English persecution.

Arriving in

Paris,

It does not require a long residence to perceive and acknowledge that it really deserves the reputation of the gayest city in the world; for, truly, it is a gay city, and the people themselves are very gay. For the most part, it is a grand and beautiful city, and no small credit of this is due, no matter what were his faults, to the good taste, energy and judgment of the late Napoleon III. The public places, squares and drives are the finest in Europe. The city, even to-day, notwithstanding the terrible damage done by the diabolic Communists, is extremely rich in glorious monuments, superb palaces, grand public edifices, unrivalled gardens and museums, and last, though certainly not least, immense and admirably constructed churches, perpetual monuments of the faith and piety of the people. To visit but one of these, the grand old Cathedral of Notre Dame, which dates from the twelfth century, and to examine closely its countless beauties of paintings and architecture, its precious treasures and inestimable relics, its thirty-seven beautiful chapels, with their richly adorned altars, would indeed require, and fully repay, several days' inspection. There are five grand, spacious aisles, and nearly three hundred columns support this majestic edifice. This is the grand old cathedral which, in the terrible Reign of Terror in 1793, was desecrated by the so-called lovers of "liberty, equality and fraternity," the enemies of God and man, of religion and morality, who, dead to all shame, set up an infamous woman on its high altar as the most worshipful Goddess of Reason.

Many other noble and stately edifices are to be found in this great city, such as for instance, the Church of St. Sulpice, the Madeleine, the Hotel des Invalides, and almost countless others that would amply repay the careful examination of the lovers of art, the admirers of antiquity, and the true, genuine Christian, rich in the possession of the greatest of treasures—the good old Catholic faith.

In visiting these grand, venerable cathedrals of Europe, we behold, in the strongest light—the wonder-inspiring monuments of our predecessors in the faith—that faith which not only enlightened and sanctified, but also refined, beautified and civilized Europe.

Talk of the darkness of the Middle Ages, and then visit, if you may, unmoved, and unconvinced of your want of truth and justice, those immense and superb cathedrals and abbeys, adorned with everything that is most precious in art, the grandest specimens of architecture the world ever saw, and which, with all its boasted progress in civilization, this present age has never been able to rival, much less to surpass.

The ages in which those noble monuments of piety and zeal were erected, were the grand old ages of Catholic faith. The people of those times may be considered by many in our days, as having been rude, ignorant and uncivilized; they had no telegraph wires nor means of rapid transit, no railroads nor steamboats, yet, with all their faults, real or imaginary, they had an abiding, unshaken faith in God and in His Church; they had a most ardent love for "*the beauty of His house and the place wherein His glory dwelleth*," and they gave most substantial proofs of it by acts of the most noble devotion and boundless liberality. They certainly did not worship to such a debasing degree as in our times, the *mighty dollar*, and they spared no effort nor expense to render unto God a becoming reverence and worship.

After a long journey from Paris, I arrived on the eve of "*Corpus Christi*" at

LOURDES,

the now world-famous shrine of the Immaculate Queen of Heaven. Lourdes is a quaint, romantic looking town, situated in the southern part of France, not far from the Spanish borders, in sight of the grand old mountains, the perpetually snow-topped Pyrenees. Every train that arrives brings its quota of pilgrims, whilst the main roads leading into the town are lined with humble peasants and the pious inhabitants of the neighboring villages, all tending towards the same point of attraction—the mysterious Grotto, as is evident from their religious demeanor and recollected air.

Sometimes whole congregations come in pilgrimage to the holy shrine, with their venerable pastors at their head, the young and the old, the little ones dressed in white, the aged mountaineers with their iron-shod staffs, their hardy faces betokening the purity and health of their mountain air, and the humble matrons, with their picturesque costumes, some with pure white and others with bright red "*capulets*" or head dress—all numbering their beads or chanting solemnly the responses to the Litany of Our Lady. A more beautiful or touching sight could not be conceived. The place itself, where the Grotto is situated, and its surroundings, cannot be surpassed for the beauty, variety and grandeur of its lovely scenery. The quaint old rocks of Massabielle, at the foot of which nature itself planned a niche for Our Lady's shrine; the miraculous stream which constantly gushes forth from its side; the lovely statue which occupies the consecrated spot where stood the wonderful vision; the numerous waxen tapers large and small, perpetually renewed and kept lighted by pious hands; the kneeling multitude in grateful heartfelt prayer; the stern-looking old castle of the Middle Ages—the key and stronghold of the Pyrenees, keeping watch over the humble worshipers below; the murmur of the waters of the Gave flowing through the peaceful, romantic valleys, whilst from afar are wafted on the balmy air the sounds of still distant pilgrims chanting pious canticles as they wend their way towards the hallowed shrine; all give but a faint idea of a scene the charm of which can never fade from one's remembrance.

Then the magnificent marble church, on the summit of the Massabielle rocks, which sprang up, as it were, by magic, and was built by the generous offerings of the grateful clients of Mary Immaculate. It is a truly grand and noble testimony to the piety and faith of a Christian people, and of their ardent devotion to the Mother of the Redeemer. This grand edifice cost over two millions of francs, and is a striking proof of the great sacrifices a devout people will make in order to show their gratitude to their most powerful intercessor with God.

What a charming sight to behold so many generous-hearted Christians engaged in earnest devotion, so many pilgrims to the holy shrine, of different ages and stations in life, hundreds of whom have walked in pious procession from their various parishes, ten, twenty or thirty miles distant! It is a pleasure to see them, after they have satisfied their devotion, spread themselves in friendly groups along the verdant banks of the busy stream, quietly enjoying their modest repast, after a long and fatiguing journey. I remember remaining awake one night listening to the soul-inspiring chants of constantly arriving bands of pilgrims, and seeing from afar the glimmer of their tapers and torches.

En passant, I may say that amongst the numerous splendid banners that adorn the church at Lourdes, and which are placed therein to represent the various dioceses or countries from which they were sent, the beautiful banner brought by our American pilgrims holds a conspicuous place, as also the American flag, blessed by our Holy Father, the Pope, and presented by the students of Georgetown College. No band of pilgrims were ever received with so much honor and every demonstration of respect, as were the members of the first American pilgrimage to the shrine of Mary Immaculate, at Lourdes, and to that of the Holy Apostles at Rome, venerating also, in the person of the great and glorious Pius IX, the humble successor of the chief of the apostolic band.

Pilgrimages

are public manifestations of faith. Their origin dates to apostolic times, for the faithful ever loved to linger around such places as were consecrated by the labors and sufferings of their beloved Redeemer, and of those who followed more closely in His sacred footsteps.

It seems to be a sort of instinct of the human heart to go abroad in search of knowledge, light and wisdom. The wisest amongst the pagans made pilgrimages in search of knowledge and of moral counsel. Pythagoras went to Egypt to visit the temples of Crete; so also did Solon. There likewise Plato went to consult with the priests.

But religion alone can present such motives for pilgrimages as will sanctify and fully satisfy those who undertake them. When entered into under the guidance of the Church, and with proper dispositions, they are a most powerful means of increasing or awakening faith, and acquiring abundance of holy graces.

The first pilgrimage we read of is mentioned in the Gospel, where we learn that multitudes of people went out into the desert to behold the first great hermit of the New Law, St. John the Baptist, and to listen to the burning words of his heaven-given eloquence.

Even in the very first ages of Christianity, those places were always held sacred where lived the saints, or where the martyrs bled for the faith; and there the faithful would assemble to pray with earnest and soul-inspiring devotion. "If I were free from ecclesiastical cares, and had sufficient health," said St. John Chrysostom, "nothing should prevent me from making a pilgrimage to the chains of St. Paul and his prison." (Hom. V, in Job.)

Truly, as Father Faber beautifully remarked: "The earth has a Catholic geography as well as a moral and physical one."

It was my great happiness to celebrate the holy sacrifice of the Mass on the beautiful feast of

"*Corpus Christi*," in one of the small chapels of the magnificent church directly over the blessed grotto. It was also with heartfelt pleasure I made the acquaintance of the holy and venerable parish priest of Lourdes, Monsignore Peyramale, who was the father confessor and faithful protector of the pure and innocent Bernardette Soubirons, to whom the Most Holy Virgin appeared eighteen times in the wonderful grotto. I visited the poor and humble house wherein the blessed maiden was born, and conversed with her sister and family. Bernadette herself is now about thirty-one years of age, and is a Sister of Charity in a convent at Nevers, where she leads a very humble, retired life, unconscious of the great religious excitement and awakening of which she was made the instrumentality in the hands of God. For most truly it was His work, and "*the weak ones of this world doth He choose that He may confound the strong.*" This great truth was fully verified in this poor, innocent, humble, unlettered child, whom He chose to make known to the world the wonderful power of the Immaculate Queen of Heaven; and this was miraculously effected, notwithstanding the powerful opposition of the civil authorities, the scepticism of the many, and the uncompromising stand of those in ecclesiastical position. The reality of the supernatural apparition was verified by the miraculous spring of water from the blessed rock, and by the undeniable character of the most astounding miracles performed at the shrine, thus baffling all human science, and proving, beyond possibility of reasonable doubt, the intervention of the supernatural.

After leaving Lourdes and returning by a branch road to the pretty town of Tarbes, the episcopal see to which Lourdes belongs, we take the train for Toulouse and Marseilles.

Toulouse

is a fine, large and important city, and is remarkable for its well buit quays and grand promenades, which I saw crowded with the gay and lively inhabitants.

Marseilles,

an old seaport town on the Mediterranean, is, for the most part, a well built city, with a great deal of order and regularity in its fine, wide avenues and thoroughfares, and is noted for the elegance and solidity of its edifices. Its principal avenue, which is beautifully laid out with noble lines of trees, and adorned with fountains, can favorably compare with the finest in Paris itself.

The evening I arrived in this beautiful city, the streets were crowded with its gay inhabitants, who are more remarkable for their fine, handsome appearance than those of most other cities in lovely France. They were all dressed in holiday attire, and were celebrating the octave of *Corpus Christi*. All the principal streets, and more especially the main avenues, were adorned with every sort of banners and flags of various dimensions, many of which were of fine texture and beautiful design. The private dwellings and public edifices were also decorated in good taste, and in proportion to the wealth of the occupiers or proprietors. Here and there were beautiful niches with elegant statues, and temporary altars fitted up and adorned for the occasion, in honor of the Adorable Sacrament. Through these avenues marched one of the grandest and most solemn processions on which my eyes ever rested. First came a large number of the loveliest and most beautiful little girls, tastefully dressed in white, and carrying bouquets of most fragrant flowers, preceded by a grand brass band; then came young ladies and gentlemen belonging to various sodalities, followed by venerable old men and women, many of whom were of extreme old age ; then numerous acolythes with swinging censers; ecclesiastics, according to their rank, with gorgeous vestments, and lastly a richly robed prelate, bearing aloft, under a canopy of gold, the brilliantly gemmed ostensorium with the Blessed Sacrament. It was a procession worthy of France in its palmiest days, but the glory of the scene was diminished by perceiving only too clearly an evident lack of practical faith in many of the beholders.

The revolutions of the past have not failed to leave their damaging effect on the devotion of many of the inhabitants of that beautiful seaport town. They are not, however, ungrateful, as a stranger may plainly see by the grand monument which they erected in one of their public squares to one of their former bishops, who died a martyr to charity during a terrible plague that infected that city.

After leaving Marseilles, the cars take you for a very considerable distance along the shore of the Mediterranean, thus affording many charming and varied views of scenery, until you reach

Florence,

The "City of Flowers," as its name denotes, formerly an Etruscan city, which sent ambassadors to Rome in the time of Tiberius. It is situated on the Arno, at quite a distance from the sea, at the foot of the sub-Alpine mountains. In the thirteenth century Florence was most remarkable and distinguished for its progress in architecture.

In that age the great architect, Arnolfo di Cambio, began the construction of the grand *duomo* or cathedral and the famous Church of "Sancta Croce," the Westminister Abbey of Italy. About the same time flourished Giotto, who is considered the founder of the Italian style of painting. In this city may be seen the home of Dante, the immortal poet, the house wherein Michael Angelo labored at his models, and the habitation of Galileo. There are several fine promenades and boulevards. A splendid view of the city and its charming surroundings can be had from the top of the old tower outside the city limits, once occupied by the famous astronomer, Galileo, as his observatory.

The wonderful and strikingly grand baptistery of St. John, (where all the children of Florence receive the sacred right of baptism) is generally believed to have been an old pagan temple, dedicated to Mars, the God of War, and dates back to the close of the fifth century. It has three superbly-wrought gates of bronze, which Michael

Angelo declared were worthy of being the portals of Paradise, one of which has bas-reliefs representing scenes in the life of St. John the Baptist; another illustrates the life of our Lord to the time of His ascension; and the third (by Ghiberti) depicts several remarkable events of the Old Testament. This baptistery is adorned with columns of porphyry, and the interior with rich mosaic work. Every year, on the feast of St. John, there is exhibited a solid silver altar, with heavy bas-reliefs representing scenes in the life of the great Precursor. It is the work of several distinguished artists, and was commenced in the year A. D. 1366 and completed in 1480, one hundred and fourteen years having been consumed in its execution.

The Church of the Holy Cross (Sancta Croce), which has so many monuments and tombs of illustrious men, is called the Florentine Pantheon. I counted as many as fourteen chapels, besides a number of private altars, over twenty massive tombs, and almost innumerable paintings, statues and frescoes. It was begun towards the close of the thirteenth century and finished towards the middle of the fifteenth. It contains the tomb of Michael Angelo, a monument erected to Dante, the tomb of Alfieri, and the Corsini monument.

The celebrated Chapel de Medicis, attached to the Church of San Lorenzo, is worthy of the most serious examination. It is of an octagonal shape, adorned on the interior with the richest and most precious stones—agate, lapis lazuli and jasper—and contains the tombs of the powerful and famous Medici family. This chapel is estimated to have cost about five millions of dollars.

The famous Medicean Gallery, to visit which with profit and advantage would require a number of days, is certainly one of the largest and grandest in the world. It contains original works of every school of painting; three hundred and fifty-four portraits of painters, executed by themselves; over five hundred paintings of illustrious men; the most complete collection of the busts of Roman emperors, of ancient and modern statuary; twenty-two thousand original designs, and thirty-three thousand medals, cameos, vases and other objects of antiquity.

Truly, Florence is exceedingly rich in treasures of art and objects of interest to the traveller, so that it is a favorite resort for tourists from distant lands.

Italy is indeed a most charming country—the delight of artists and of poets, the favorite land of painters, sculptors and antiquarians, the classic land of liberty.

Beauty in every shape and form is here displayed. The sky with its multiform shades of color, of refined brilliancy and incomparable magnificence; the serenity of its sweetly-perfumed atmosphere; the varied beauties of scenery, the vine clad hills, the blooming orchards, the picturesque valleys, the wayside shrines, the gorgeous churches, the magnificent basilicas; and connected with all these, clinging to each ruin, attached to every stream and lake, forest and woodland scene, the histories of its glorious past, altogether make it a land of ever-deepening interest to every traveller from a distant clime.

In emerging from its quaint old towns or more modernized cities, in travelling over its fertile plains, admiring the most generous hand of nature lavishing so many and such varied beauties on its noble outline of country, the Christian tourist is constantly reminded of a still more beauteous land to which the aspirations of his soul should tend, by the frequent signs of Catholic faith he meets with in his pleasant wanderings; for, whether his course lead him by the lofty mountain-top, the secluded valley or more lively town, he cannot fail to perceive the sign of man's salvation on the hillside, the frescoed wall in honor of the Immaculate Virgin, or rustic shrine with simple statue adorned, to elevate his thoughts and bless as well as cheer him on his journey.

"As usual, on Italian waysides," says Nathaniel Hawthorne, we pass "great, black crosses, hung with all the instruments of the sacred agony and passion; there were the crown of thorns, the hammer and nails, the pinchers, the spear, the sponge; and perched over the whole, the cock that crowed to Saint Peter's remorseful conscience. Thus, while the fertile scene showed the never-failing beneficence of the Creator towards man in his transitory state, these symbols reminded each wayfarer of the Saviour's infinitely greater love for him as an immortal spirit." "These shrines were everywhere; under arched niches, or in little pent-houses with a brick-tiled roof, just large enough to shelter them; or perhaps in some bit of old Roman masonry, the founders of which had died before the Advent; or in the wall of a country inn or farm-house, or at the midway point of a bridge, or in the shallow cavity of a natural rock, or high upward in the deep cuts of the road. . . . It was beautiful to observe, indeed, how tender was the soul of man and woman towards the Virgin Mother, in recognition of the tenderness which, as their faith taught them, she immortally cherishes towards all human souls. In the wire-work screen, before each shrine, hung offerings of roses, or whatever flower was the sweetest and most seasonable."

But how much deeper becomes our emotion, how far more intensified our feelings of awe and admiration, as we gradually approach

ROME

itself—the Eternal City—the "City of the Soul," the very mention of which summons to our minds the recollections of a history the most wonderful in the annals of the human race. Rome—that city around which cluster the memories of all that was great, grand, glorious and majestic in pagandom, all that is noble, heroic, elevating and civilizing in Christiandom. Surely no other city in the world ever held or shall hold the position in history, which she occupied and still continues to occupy, notwithstanding the lapse of centuries and the ruin of empire.

What Rome was to the ancient world, Rome is still to the modern world, whether in the height of power or the lowliness of distress, the city which attracts the gaze and repays the attention of every lover of the true, the grand, the beautiful and the sublime.

How much more affecting for the Christian beholder, when he gazes for the first time on that grand old city, built on the eternal hills, with its hundreds of holy temples, gigantic ruins, lofty palaces, magnificent basilicas, above which towers in grandeur and majesty the incomparable dome of St. Peter's, all bathed in the most glorious sunshine!

How soul-inspiring when he thinks of its wondrous history, the glorious achievements of its heroic age, the splendor and power of its days of empire, the matchless eloquence of its orators, the charming periods of its poets, the invincible bravery of its fearless citizens!

His mind tenderly reverts to the first feeble glimmerings of divine faith amidst the universal moral darkness that prevailed in this mighty seat of empire; the humble entrance of its first apostles; the sowing of the seed of Gospel truth, and the gradual unfolding of Christ's unfading banner on the very bulwark of paganism.

Then it is that Rome becomes more sacred in his eyes than any glories of mere worldly history can make it, by the thought of its thousands of martyrs, belonging to every station in life—the venerable senator, the princely maiden, the humble matron, the dauntless soldier, the tender virgin—meeting death in the horrible arena, in presence of Rome's hundred thousand scoffers; thrown as food to the wild beasts; tortured and racked in every limb, or smeared with pitch to serve as burning torches for an impious populace. Surely every stone and monument, ruin and shrine become hallowed in his eyes as relics of the glorious ages of Christian martyrdom.

But when our eyes rest on the majestic

St. Peter's,

"the cathedral of all Christendom," as Wendell Phillips beautifully terms it, the grandest temple ever erected by the hands of man to the worship of the only true God, the soul is overpowered by a variety of thrilling sensations, the sense of overpowering grandeur, vast dimension, impressive awe, and sublimity of conception. It is to this unrivaled basilica that the pilgrim or tourist first directs his steps, on his arrival in the Eternal City. So immense is it, so wonderfully grand and majestic, that not until you have made repeated visits, can you form any true idea of its astonishing dimensions. This arises from the most admirable proportions, according to which the entire edifice is constructed.

> "Enter; its grandeur overwhelms thee not;
> And why? It is not lessened, but thy mind,
> Expanded by the genius of the spot,
> Has grown colossal, and can only find
> A fit abode wherein appear enshrined
> Thy hopes of immortality."

It is only then, after several visits and close inspection, that the mind can take in its immensity, can discern more faithfully the strictest proportion of the entire, and appreciate the wondrous beauty of each statue, pillar, altar and mosaic. After walking for hours through this largest, richest and grandest of human temples, the predominating sensation is one of undefinable awe, overpowering all the senses, so impressed do we become with the divine majesty which seems to pervade the whole, blessing the noblest work of man's genius, so befittingly dedicated to the worship of the Supreme Architect of the universe.

St. Peter's stands on the site of the Circus of Nero, where thousands of Christians suffered martyrdom, and where St. Peter was buried. Here Constantine the Great built a basilica which lasted for many ages, until the present edifice was begun on the same site, about the beginning of the sixteenth century. The main building is estimated to have cost about fifty millions of dollars. The vestry, which was built by Pius VI, cost a million.

There are conflicting statements with regard to the exact dimensions, but it is about 620 or 650 feet in length on the exterior, 209 to 220 in breadth, and 465 to the top of the cross. The ball on which the cross is placed is so large as to be capable of holding sixteen persons at a time; and on the roof is a town in miniature, a little St. Petersburg it might be called, where a large number of workmen reside. If you stand near the high altar and look down towards the main portal, and watch the diminutive-looking figures of those who are but just entering, it will give some satisfactory idea of the extreme length of the edifice.

The walls and pavement are of purest marble. There are 290 windows, 390 statues, 46 altars and 748 columns. The grand canopy over the main altar (where only the Pope himself officiates on great festivals) is 98 feet in height. Below it is the tomb or "*confessio*" of St. Peter, as it is called. The descent to it is by a double marble staircase. Here, at the very fountain-head, as I might well call it, of Catholic unity, I had the inestimable privilege of offering up the holy sacrifice of the

Mass. Nearly one hundred lamps of silver and gold are constantly kept burning before this hallowed shrine. There are confessionals here and there throughout the edifice, where confessions are heard in all the principal languages of the earth. Truly, it may be called the cathedral of all Christiandom. It was consecrated by Urban VIII, on the 18th of November, 1626, the 1300th anniversary of the dedication of the former basilica by Pope St. Sylvester.

Never can I forget the 21st of June, 1874, the twenty-ninth anniversary of the coronation of Our Holy Father, Pope Pius IX, when this grandest of temples resounded to the solemn yet most joyous chant of the *Te Deum*, sung by thirty thousand voices in thanksgiving to the Almighty for the wonderfully prolonged pontificate of the great and saintly Pius IX, whom may God still longer preserve to behold the triumph of that church for which he has suffered so much.

After visiting St. Peter's, the most wondrous

work of architecture of modern times, we naturally direct our steps toward the

Colosseum,

the most magnificent ruin of Imperial Rome. There it stands in all its awe-inspiring immensity, its stately grandeur, its hoary antiquity, "a noble wreck in ruinous perfection," as Byron quaintly terms it, the most lasting monument of the power, the glory, the magnificence of proud, imperious Rome, the once haughty mistress of the world. Being the largest, most massive and stately amphitheatre the world ever saw, it recalls to the mind the proud capital of the world in all the splendor of its imperial majesty, lording it over the entire earth, claiming the tribute of every nation, tribe and people, and forcing all to contribute to its pomp, pride, luxury and licentiousness. And, yet, whilst this imperishable structure recalls the days of its power, wealth, amusements and extravagance, it stands, nevertheless, an undying memorial of its barbarity, its cruelty, its injustice, and its insatiable thirst for human blood, as witnessed in its gladiatorial combats and terrible persecutions.

The Colosseum is an everlasting monument of pagan power, cruelty and barbarity, and, at the same time, a most glorious memorial of the civilizing character of Christianity, its invincible heroism and undying faith; for here, in this vast amphitheatre, where tier rises upon tier, and grandeur vies with grandeur, all that was powerful, fair and noble amongst the great Roman people used to assemble, on days of public rejoicing, to feast their eyes on the terrible, bloody scenes of the arena, where men were forced to struggle with the fierce animals of the forest or to enter into single combat with their fellowmen; where the vanquished princes, nobles and brave warriors of other nations met with a cruel death, and where the undaunted followers of Christ were cast to the wild beasts, slowly burned on the gridiron, or tortured to death by the most ingenious devices of hatred and cruelty.

This immense structure was commenced by the Emperor Vespasian, in A.D. 72, and was finished by Titus in A.D. 80. Thirty thousand Jews, who were brought captive from Jerusalem, were daily employed in its construction. It is estimated that it used to accommodate one hundred thousand persons at a time; and though eighteen centuries have rolled by since it was erected, though it was often disfigured by storm and shell, shaken by earthquakes, barricaded by armies, despoiled by princes and nobles, it still stands, the noblest, grandest ruin of ancient Rome.

> The gladiator's bloody circus stands,
> A noble wreck, in ruinous perfection!
> While Cæsar's chambers and the Augustan halls
> Grovel on earth in indistinct decay;
> And thou didst shine, thou rolling moon, upon
> All this, and cast a wide and tender light,
> Which softened down the hoar austerity
> Of rugged desolation, and filled up,

As 'twere anew, the gaps of centuries,
Leaving that beautiful which still was so,
And making that which was not, till the place
Became religion, and the heart ran o'er
With silent worship of the great of old.
     —*Byron's* "*Manfred.*"

The city of Rome has as many churches as there are days in the year, each being, as Gerbet says, "the monumental expression of some mystery of faith, or of some great example of virtue drawn from the lives of the saints; so that if we could embrace them in view all at once, we should have before our eyes the plan of the whole of Religion." (*Esquisse de Rome Chretienne.*)

The most important church after that of St. Peter is St. John Lateran, which has been from the time of Constantine the Great, the principal church of Rome and the world, "*omnium urbis et orbis ecclesiarum mater et caput,*" where are preserved the heads of St. Peter and St. Paul. It was overthrown by earthquake, A.D. 896, reconstructed in the year 904, burnt down in 1308, and erected again by Pope Clement V, and decorated under succeeding Pontiffs. The high altar (at which only the Pope officiates on the most solemn feasts) contains a wooden table, taken from the Catacombs, which was used as an altar by St. Peter. In this edifice the Pope is crowned; and from the central upper loggia of this Basilica, he pronounces the Papal benediction on Ascension day.

The Liberian Basilica, *Sancta Maria Maggiore*, was built in honor of the Virgin Mary by Pope Liberius, A.D. 352, on the spot where was found a miraculous deposit of snow, indicating the place pointed out in a vision to the Pope and the Roman Patrician Johannes; hence it is sometimes called "Sancta Maria ad Nives." Mosaics of the fifth century represent events in the Old and New Testaments. There is a sarcophagus in this church containing the remains of St. Matthew; also the tombs of Nicholas IV (1292) and Clement IV (A.D. 1669). The altar in the Borghese Chapel is decorated with lapis lazuli and agate, and possesses a most ancient miraculous painting of the Blessed Virgin (now almost black with age), said to have been painted by St. Luke. It was carried in procession through the city of Rome by St. George I, in A.D. 590, and also in the year 1860, to obtain the intercession of the most Holy Virgin.

The crypt beneath contains the tombs of the famous Borghese family. "In front of and beneath the high altar, Pius IX has lately been preparing his own monument, by constructing a splendid chamber approached by staircases, and lined with the most precious alabaster and marbles." (A. J. Hare.)

A most interesting church to visit is that of

Santo Lorenzo,

outside the walls of Rome, the burial place of St. Lawrence the Deacon and Martyr. Here was formerly a basilica built by Constantine. The interior of the present edifice consists of two parts, the more modern of which dating from the time of Honorius III (13th century) is supported by twenty-two ancient columns of granite. At the extremity of the left aisle, a staircase descends to the lower chapel and the Catacombs. You descend by seven marble steps to the *Confessio*, as it is called, where are the remains of the two holy deacons, St. Stephen the first martyr, and St. Lawrence. Twelve magnificent fluted columns support the antique entablature.

Attached to this basilica, is a beautiful cemetery, the chief burial ground of Rome, where may be seen a magnificent monument representing St. Peter and a kneeling knight, erected by Pope Pius IX in 1870, in honor of the fallen heroes of Mentana (1867). The civil authorities have, of late, placed a mean slab at the base of this monument, to show their hatred for the "Papal Mercenaries," as they contemptuously call the late gallant zouaves.

The Catacombs attached to this venerated basilica are worthy of examination, but, notwithstanding the deep interest they cannot fail to excite, it would not be at all very prudent, during the warm season, to spend much time in investigation, as a person would be very liable to an attack of the terrible Roman fever, on account of the dampness and chilliness of these last resting-places of the primitive Christians.

The best preserved of all the ancient edifices is the Pantheon, a temple formerly dedicated to all the gods of Rome, but, since the beginning of the seventh century (Pope Boniface, A.D. 610) solemnly consecrated to all the saints in heaven. It was built by Agrippa, son-in-law of the Emperor Augustus, B.C. 27. The portico consists of sixteen granite Corinthian columns, each thirty-eight feet in height. This symmetrically constructed edifice is lighted only by an aperture in the dome. Here we see a monument which was erected to Cardinal Consalvi, Secretary of State, to Pius VII, and the tomb of Raphael.

On visiting the church of *San Pietro in Vinculi*, which was built in the fifth century by the Empess Eudoxia, I had the honor of holding in my hands, and of presenting to others who had assembled to kiss and venerate them, the chains wherewith St. Peter was bound. Here, also, I beheld, with awe and veneration, a considerable portion of the True Cross, on which our blessed Saviour hung in his death agony for man's redemption; and what produced still deeper emotion in my soul, one of the huge, fierce-looking nails with which his sacred limbs were so cruelly pierced.

I ascended the *Scala Sancta,* or Holy Staircase —twenty-eight marble steps, brought to Rome in the year 326 through the instrumentality of St. Helena, the mother of the great Constantine. They are the same identical steps that formed the entrance to the court of Pilate, to which our Redeemer was so cruelly dragged in suffering and derision. No persons are permitted to ascend except on their knees, out of reverence for the passion of our Saviour.

The most deeply interesting old church one can visit in Rome is that of

ST. CLEMENT,

which is attended by the Irish Dominicans. The present building dates partly from the ninth and partly from the twelfth century. Directly under this structure is a church of the fourth century, discovered in 1857, and, wonderful to relate, lower still is a much older structure (discovered in 1867), the very house of St. Clement, the fellow-laborer of St. Paul and the third Bishop of Rome. Here are to be found remains of rich stucco ornaments and symbolic figures, attesting the belief of the early ages of Christianity in the chief mysteries of our faith.

It is, indeed, deeply moving and affecting, as well as interesting, to visit these sanctified abodes and meeting places of the earliest Christians and martyrs, where they were accustomed to assemble in secret and attend the celebration of the most sacred mysteries. There, far below the surface of the proud city, in places which, like this I visited, seemed more like horrible dungeons than oratories, they prepared themselves by prayer, and nourished themselves with the Bread of Life, to undergo the terrible ordeal of suffering and death for the glory of their undying faith.

There the aged apostolic laborer, there the noble patrician, the venerable Roman matron and the modest, tender virgin comforted each other in prayer and counsel, and strengthened themselves for the coming conflicts by the all-powerful means of the sacraments.

What a history those old walls could tell of the heroic fortitude, the angelic piety, the divine charity, of those early Christians, and of the terrible sacrifices which they underwent in honor of their spotless faith. What a strong rebuke to the worldliness and religious indifference of our own age and the small esteem in which eternal truths are held by the great multitude of this world's admirers!

In the

Vatican,

which is in close proximity to St. Peter's, and is, you might say, a collection of palaces, containing, as it does, a number of courts, halls, chapels and various apartments, to the number of eleven thousand, is the famous Sixtine Chapel (built by Sixtus IV, in 1473), where the Pope officiates with great solemnity in Holy week. The walls are decorated by Florentine artists of the fifteenth century, representing parallel scenes in the lives of Moses and of Christ. The ceiling is most beautifully adorned with a grand pictorial work of Michael Angelo, which occupied him during twenty-two months (A.D. 1508), representing the most striking events which prefigured the advent of Christ. Most remarkable of all, however, is the painting of the Last Judgment, back of the altar, which occupied Michael Angelo during the long period of seven years.

The Vatican library has the finest collection of manuscripts in the world, twenty-four thousand in number, seventeen thousand of which are in the Latin, twelve thousand in the Oriental, and forty-five hundred in the Greek languages. The library of the Minerva has more printed volumes than the Vatican—120,000, whilst the latter has only 50,000.

Near the Capitol may be seen whatever remains of the ruins of the ancient Roman Forum; the Temple of Saturn, with eight columns tolerably well preserved; three columns of the Temple of Vespasian; the Arch of Septimus Severus; the Column of Phocas; the Julian Basilica; the Temple of Castor and Pollux. Some distance beyond are the arches of Constantine and Titus (the latter commemorating his triumph over Jerusalem), and the imperishable Colosseum.

>In many a heap the ground
>Heaves, as though Ruin, in a frantic mood,
>Had done his utmost. Here and there appears,
>As left to show *his* handiwork, not ours,
>An idle column, a half-buried arch,
>A wall of some great temple. It was once
>The Forum, whence a mandate, eagle-winged,

Went to the ends of the earth. Let us descend
Slowly. At every step much may be lost.
The very dust we tread stirs as with life,
And not the slightest breath that sends not up
Something of human grandeur. We are come,
Are now, where once the mightiest spirits met
In terrible conflict; this, while Rome was free,
The noblest theatre on this side Heaven.
—*Rogers*.

In visiting the Eternal City, its magnificent ruins, noble monuments of art and incomparable temples of religion, there is yet another sight which moves our feelings more, and causes an ecstasy of delight in the heart of the happy beholder. That is the sight of the great and saintly

POPE PIUS IX,

the Vicar of Jesus Christ, and supreme head of the Catholic Church on earth. One look at that noble, grand and venerable pontiff would repay a journey from the extremity of the earth. Pope Pius IX, the most towering figure among the greatest men of the age, "*tanquam cedrus inter Libanos, quasi cypressus in monte Sion*"—"as the cedar tree of Libanus, as the cypress on Mount Sion," pope, confessor and martyr, too, he might well be called, who has sat and ruled in the Chair of Peter longer than any of his predecessors, not excepting St. Peter himself. Of scarcely more than medium size, somewhat full in figure, clothed in a plain but pure white woolen soutane, with a face in which benevolence and majesty seem wonderfully blended; an eye full, clear, kindly, yet penetrating, and beautiful silvery hair crowning his noble brow, surely he presents an appearance that can never fade from one's remembrance. Then that lovely affability towards all, that simple yet charming gayety and winning kindness naturally gain the love as well as admiration of every beholder.

What a grand central figure he makes in the midst of his cardinals robed in scarlet, the bishops in purple, and the Swiss Guards in picturesque costume; and he, the Supreme Pontiff, the humblest and plainest, yet strikingly grand amongst all! No one, whether Protestant, Catholic or infidel, ever leaves his presence without being duly impressed with reverence for his amiable and august person. He, I can truly say, is all and even more than my fancy pictured him, and one in whom all my imaginings were realized—the grand old prisoner of the Vatican.

So strikingly remarkable is his appearance, that were he in an assembly of his bishops and cardinals, to wear the same robes as they, without any distinction of color or material, I verily believe that a stranger would naturally single him out as the chief of the whole illustrious band. His style of conversation is natural, easy, graceful, eloquent and dignified, and is always food for deep reflection. He is, in truth, the most impressive of men.

I had the pleasure of visiting the quaint old town in which he was born—*Sinigaglia* (the Sena Gallica of the ancients, which was destroyed in the civil war at the time of Pompey). It is a town of about 11,000 inhabitants. There he was born on the 13th of May, 1792. After making very successful studies at the college of Volterra, he entered the Noble Guards at the age of twenty. Some time afterwards, being afflicted with severe attacks of epilepsy, he was counseled by Pope Pius VII to make a pilgrimage to the Holy House of Loretto, where he was miraculously cured, and where, in consequence, he vowed himself to the service of God in the ecclesiastical state. Whilst at Loretto, I saw the rich presents which he bestowed on the church in thanksgiving for the great favor obtained through the intercession of Our Lady of Loretto.

Abandoning the military profession, he studied theology under the Jesuit fathers, and after his ordination to the priesthood, he took charge of an asylum called "*Tata Giovanni*," which he most generously assisted out of the revenues of his own family estate. He was soon after sent to Chili, South America, as auditor to Mgr. Muzi, Vicar Apostolic and Papal Nuncio. Some time after his return to Italy he was consecrated, in 1827, Bishop of Spoleto, where he labored with astonishing success for five years, when, to the great regret of all the inhabitants, and against their most urgent entreaties, he was transferred by Gregory XVI, in 1832, to the important see of Imola, of which Pius VII had formerly been bishop, before being raised to the papal throne.

In 1840 he was raised to the cardinalate, and on June 16th, 1846, he was elected Pope, and crowned on the 21st of the same month. Notwithstanding the astonishing liberality and almost excessive clemency of his reign, he was exiled from his dominions in the fall of 1848, and after an absence of over sixteen months, he was, to the great joy of all good Christians throughout the world, restored to his throne in April, 1850, through the valor and devotedness of the French army. Although left comparatively in peace for some years, during which he labored most arduously and successfully, not only in improving and beautifying the city of Rome, but also in guarding, with most zealous attention, the interests of the universal

Church, his life has been one of trial, sorrow and conflict. Firm, courageous and reliant, however, with unshaken trust in God and in the justice of his cause, he stands to-day the most venerable and venerated object in the living history of the Church—the undaunted hero of the Vatican.

Sad, indeed, is the change that has come over Rome in the last few years; change in its government, in many of the people in consequence of the additions to their number of the revolutionists and their followers; change as to the absence of that peace, and order, and security for life and person that prevailed under the beneficent rule of the Pope. This sad alteration is quickly discernible, especially to those who visited Rome before the new *regimé* was violently introduced, and it has been well described by Augustus J. C. Hare (not a member of our faith), in his latest work entitled "Days Near Rome," from which I cull the following extract confirmatory of my declaration:

"In Rome, now, the ancient characteristics

have entirely perished, having been swept away in three years in a manner which sounds incredible, and which would have seemed incredible beforehand. And, while acknowledging certain beneficial changes (!) introduced by the present government, it is not only the artist who will recognize that much of the interest, and as much as possible of the beauty of the "Eternal City" has been destroyed. Not only has all trace of costume perished, together with the mediæval figures and splendid dresses which belonged to the Papal Court, and walked in the footsteps of crimson Cardinals; but all the gorgeous religious ceremonies, all the processions, and benedictions, and sermons preached by the shrines of martyrs, have ceased to exist. Even the time-honored *Pifferari* have been chased from Rome by the present government as a public nuisance. The closing of so many convents and the robbery of the dowries of so many nuns (given on their entrance in the same sense in which a marriage portion is given), has not only been an act of crying injustice in itself, which even the strongest Protestants must feel, but while it has flooded the streets with starving, helpless or infirm persons, who subsisted on the daily convent dole of coarse bread and soup, it has thrown thousands of helpless ladies, who believed themselves provided for during their lives (and by their own families), into a state of utter destitution, for the relief of which the miserable and irregularly paid pension of a few pence a day appointed by the government sounds merely like a mockery."

This is a true and candid description of the melancholy state to which so many pious *religieuses* have been reduced, not only in Rome, but throughout the whole of Italy, by the unjust laws and miserable persecution of the usurping government.

Nor has religion alone suffered; for art and architecture will be sad losers by the change of rulers, as this candid writer admits: " Many famous antiquarian memorials have disappeared, together with other well-known buildings, of which the interest was confined to Papal times.

The Agger of Servius Tullius and the ruined Ponte Salara have been swept away. The incomparable view from the Ponte Rotto has been blocked out, the trees on the Aventine and the woods of Monte Mario have been cut down. The Villa Negroni-Massimo, the most beautiful of Roman gardens, with the grandest of old orange avenues, and glorious groves of cypresses amid which Horace was buried—a villa whose terraces dated from the time when it belonged to Mæcenas, and which was replete with recollections of the romantic story of Vittoria Accorambuoni, of Donna Camilla Perretti and of Alfieri, has been ruthlessly and utterly ploughed up, so that not a trace of it is left. Even this, however, is as nothing compared with the entire destruction of the beauty and charm of the grandest of the buildings which remain. . . . Should the present state of things continue much longer, and especially should Signor Rosa remain in power, the whole beauty of Rome will have disappeared, except that which the Princes guard in their villas, and that which the everlasting hills and the glowing Campagna can never fail to display."

After leaving the Eternal City, and taking a farewell look at all its grandeur, I journeyed towards

LORETTO,

to visit the Holy House of Nazereth, in which the holiest of families—Jesus, Mary and Joseph—dwelt for so many years together, unknown to the world, but in the closest union with Heaven. In this extremely poor, humble, but blessed cabin, was born Mary, the Immaculate Mother of God; here the angel Gabriel announced unto her the incarnation of the Son of God about to be accomplished in her womb; here the Saviour, His mother, and his foster-father, St. Joseph, dwelt in poverty and obscurity, until He entered on His divine and public mission.

The history of the "Holy House" is indeed most wonderful and miraculous; but it rests on the most trustworthy foundations. Although the town of Nazereth was ravaged in the first century by the troops of Titus and Vespasian, the "Holy House" escaped destruction; but when the pious Empress Helena, the mother of Constantine the Great, made a pilgrimage to the Holy Land (A.D. 307), and visited Bethlehem, Calvary and the Holy Sepulchre, on proceeding to Nazareth she found the Holy House amid a mass of ruins.

Leaving the poor, but sacred building undisturbed, and causing to be placed therein the table or temporary altar on which the Apostles offered up the Holy Sacrifice, she gave orders for the erection of a grand and magnificent temple, on the marble façade of which was engraved these words: "*Hac est ara, in qua primo jactum est humanæ salutis fundamentum.*" "This is the temple in which was first laid the foundation of man's salvation."

This grand basilica surrounding the Holy House was still in existence when St. Louis, King of France, after having been freed from captivity, went on foot, as an humble pilgrim, from Mount Thabor, to venerate the sacred dwelling on the feast of the Annunciation, March 25, 1252, and assisted at the holy sacrifice of the mass celebrated therein by the legate of the Holy See, Odo, Bishop of Frascati.

Towards the end of the thirteenth century the whole country in and around Galilee was ravaged and destroyed by the Caliph of Egypt, but God's providence rested on the Holy House, and to preserve it from the desecration of the Saracens it was miraculously transported by the instrumentality of angels, first to Dalmatia, and finally to Loretto, in Italy, in the year 1294.

It was found to rest without foundations or support of any kind, on uneven ground, in a part of the country where there was no habitation or dwelling of any sort. The little structure bore a very ancient appearance; the stones were of such a peculiar kind as not to be found in the whole country, and the boards were of an azure color and divided into little squares; inside was a small altar attached to the wall, also an old wooden Greek cross and a strange-looking statue of the Virgin and Child.

No one could account for the wondrous occurrence, until it was revealed to some very devout persons that it was the Holy House of Nazereth which was thus miraculously transferred. Its dimensions were then taken, and commissioners were sent by the civil and ecclesiastical authorities to the Holy Land, to inquire into the history of the House. On their arrival at Nazereth they found only the original foundation remaining, and after taking the exact dimensions into consideration, the length, breadth and thickness, the style of building and the quality of the stones, they found that everything perfectly corresponded with the miraculously-transferred house at Loretto.

The present magnificent temple by which the Holy House is enclosed was built in the time of Paul II (fifteenth century), and is adorned with numerous chapels, nearly every one of which possesses some remarkable work of art.

The walls of the Holy House itself are thirteen feet three inches in height, fourteen inches thick, twenty-nine feet four inches in length, and twelve feet eight inches wide. In the interior is a very old cedar-wood statue of the Blessed Virgin and Child, which dates back to the times of the Apostles. It is covered with diamonds and precious stones of marvellous beauty and richness. Popes and bishops, kings and queens, donated to the Holy House the most precious gifts and ornaments, as an earnest of their faith and devotion. Our own most glorious Pontiff, Pius IX, presented a solid gold chalice, and celebrated mass several times in the blessed abode. His illustrious predecessors, Pius VII and Pius VIII, also presented solid gold chalices to the basilica.

For five hundred years has the Holy House been venerated at Loretto, and thousands and hundreds of thousands have visited it with every mark of the most soul-inspiring devotion. Several Popes have done all in their power to confirm the devotion of the people; have enriched it with the most precious indulgences and privileges, and testified their own veneration by very valuable gifts. No less than one hundred saints and beatified servants of God have visited this holy shrine with ardent faith and heartfelt devotion.

It was my great happiness to celebrate the Holy Sacrifice of the Mass within these hallowed precincts. When I was vested for Mass, a brightly uniformed old cavalier, who is constantly on duty with cocked hat and drawn sword immediately preceded me, and effected an entrance amidst the crowd of worshippers.

It would be impossible to describe the variety and intensity of the emotions that fill the souls of those who pray within these blessed walls, and that which more particularly impress one who celebrates the Holy Sacrifice, where the Divine Victim prepared Himself for His oblation by so many years of prayer, labor and retirement in that small, poor, obscure dwelling. Such joys and such a privilege more than compensate for any length of journey or tediousness of travel and leave an unfading remembrance of a pleasure more than earthly.

Having freed myself by small donations from the innumerable beggars that swarm around this sacred place, I drove, in company with the Rev. Dr. Crager, O.S.F., formerly of Albany, N. Y., and now attached to the Basilica as Confessor, to Castelfidardo, where the Papal troops so nobly distinguished themselves, though fighting against an overwhelming number of the Italian usurpers.

There is a grand, magnificent and widely extended view from the heights, with a view of the noble Adriatic, and of lovely, fertile plains, but now, alas! poverty-stricken country. The people are overburdened and oppressed with taxes, and there is but little security for life or property. Revolution has sadly changed this country, on which nature has lavished its charms, and religion, its manifold blessings.

Leaving Loretto, I proceeded to one of the loveliest cities in Europe,

VENICE,

the Queen of the Sea. It is formed of a cluster of islands, over one hundred in number, and really seems to rest on the waves. It is the only city where you will find no horses or carriages, there being in fact scarcely any streets, but marine thoroughfares; the finest and most important being the Grand Canal, dividing the city into two almost equal parts, and one hundred and forty-six smaller canals, along which glide, at all hours of the day and night, whether for business or pleasure, graceful gondolas skillfully managed by grave-looking gondoliers.

As the poet, Rogers, describes it:

> "There is a glorious city in the sea;
> The sea is in the broad, the narrow streets,
> Ebbing and flowing; and the salt sea-weed
> Clings to the marble of her palaces.
> No track of man, no footsteps to and fro,

> Lead to her gates. The path lies o'er the sea,
> Invisible; and from the land we went
> As to a floating city—steering in,
> And gliding up her streets as in a dream."

I scarcely know of any place where a person may spend a week or two with greater pleasure or profit than in Venice. At any hour you may engage a gondola, and, besides enjoying the pleasant sail, you may alight at any point of interest, visit some famous church or noted work of art or grand palace by the water's edge. In the evening, you may again summon your faithful gondolier, who will bear you gently and swiftly over the waters to the neighboring island of Lido, that separates the lagoon of Venice from the Adriatic; and there every evening in summer, you may, at a trifling cost, attend any one of the operatic concerts that attract so many of the Venetians from their lovely city.

Then, on your return, you see the noble city reposing majestically on the waters, with its grand palaces and the lofty domes of its many temples all brilliantly lit up and bathed in a still more glorious moonlight, casting reflections on the silver waves.

One's first visit is always paid to the Piazza and Cathedral of St. Mark. The cathedral is grand and gorgeous, and has somewhat the appearance of a Mosque; this, no doubt, owing to the façt, that a part of the structure was formed from portions taken from the temple of St. Sophia in Constantinople.

San Marco,

built in honor of St. Mark, the Evangelist, whose remains, brought with great pomp and devotion from the East, were buried here under the grand altar, was built in the eleventh century, in the Byzantine style of architecture, with additions in the fourteenth and seventeenth centuries. Above the grand portals are the celebrated bronze horses brought from Rome to Constantinople by Constantine, in the fourth century, and from the latter place to Venice, in the beginning of the thirteenth century, by Marino Zeno, when Constantinople was taken by the Crusaders. The first Napoleon admired these horses of bronze so much that he stole them from the Venetians, to whom, however, they were returned after his downfall in 1815.

This magnificent basilica defies accurate description. There is one large dome and four smaller ones, and the interior is one blaze of glory, which would be dazzling were it not that the light comes in so softly as not to overburden with too much brightness. The ceiling is of the richest mosaic work, with the ground of gold, whilst the floor is of marble in mosaic, with numbers of rich pillars of porphyry and variegated marble. The high altar is adorned with every kind of gems and precious stones.

The interior of this superb edifice is thus beautifully described by Ruskin in his famous work, "Stones of Venice:"

"There opens before us a vast cave, hewn out into the form of a cross, and divided into shadowy aisles by many pillars. Round the domes of its roof the light enters only through narrow apertures, like large stars; and here and there a ray or two from some far away casement wanders into the darkness, and casts a narrow phosphoric stream upon the waves of marble that heave and fall in a thousand colors along the floor. What else there is of light is from torches or silver lamps, burning ceaselessly in the recesses of the chapels; the roof, sheathed with gold, and the polished walls, covered with alabaster, give back at every curve and angle some feeble gleaming to the flames; and the glories round the heads of the sculptured saints flash out upon us as we pass them, and sink again into the gloom. Under foot and over head a continual succession of crowded imagery, one picture passing into another, as in a dream; forms beautiful and terrible, mixed together; dragons, and serpents, and ravening beasts of prey, and graceful birds that in the midst of them drink from running fountains and feed from vases of crystal; the passions and the pleasures of human life symbolized together, and the mystery of its redemption—for the mazes of interwoven lines and changeful pictures lead always at last to the cross, lifted and carved in every place and upon every stone, sometimes with the serpent of eternity wrapt around it, sometimes with doves beneath its arms and sweet herbage growing forth from its feet; but conspicuous most of all on the great road that crosses the church before the altar, raised in bright blazonry against the shadow of the apse."

After visiting the cathedral, the next object of greatest interest is the ducal palace, an imperishable memorial of the power, the glory, the magnificence, of Venice in its palmiest days. Here may be found some of the greatest masterpieces of art: the grand painting of Tintoretto, said to be the largest oil painting in the world; masterly sketches of Venetian history adorn the gorgeous ceilings of the council chambers (by Paul Veronese), and the portraits of the Doges, or chief into these officers of Venice, by the immortal

Titian, by Tintoretto and other most noted painters, are to be seen in this wonderfully rich edifice.

The dungeons down by the water's edge, dark, massive and fearfully gloomy, where no light was ever allowed to penetrate, and where political prisoners were once immurred, would send such a thrill through a person's frame that he would not at all be anxious to linger very long, meditating over the past, when the Council of Ten exercised such fearful and despotic power.

The Academy of Fine Arts, now established in a suppressed monastery, contains many unrivalled works of art, especially the masterpieces of the "Assumption," and "St. John in the Desert," Tintoretto's "Adam and Eve," Bellini's masterpieces, and five or six hundred more elegant and valuable works of art.

The Church of the Jesuits (now no longer in their possession) is beautifully adorned with rich and variegated marbles, and has a painting that attracts much admiration, "The Martyrdom of St. Laurence," by the great master, Titian. Gliding along the Grand Canal, within a short distance of the railway station, we enter a church built in the thirteenth century, "Santa Maria Gloriosa dei Frari," where can be seen a magnificent marble monument to Titian and the massive tomb of Canova. So Venice is, in many respects, one of the most interesting cities in the world.

After leaving beautiful Venice, the next city in which I made any considerable stay was the noble city of

MILAN,

on the river Olona, formerly the capital of Lombardy. It has a population of more than a quarter of a million inhabitants, a very flourishing, orderly, well built city, with beautiful gardens, squares and promenades. It is more especially noted for its superb duomo or cathedral, all built of white marble, even the very roof being covered with massive slabs of marble, well cemented together. There are 106 pinnacles rising in graceful proportions from the roof, above which towers a sort of obelisk, nearly 400 feet from the ground, and surmounted by a bronze statue of the Immaculate Conception. You can ascend by some hundreds of marble steps within a few feet of the summit, and only then you can form a true idea of the wondrous marvels of art that adorn every part of this magnificent structure. Here also you are blessed with a grand and most extensive view of the surrounding country, with all its Italian loveliness of scenery, over which preside, in solemn grandeur, the Alpine and Appenine mountains.

Every pinnacle, and in fact every available spot in and around the building is adorned with marble statues of saints, confessors and martyrs; and it is estimated that there are in all, interiorly and exteriorly, 7,000 marble statues, many of which, taken separately, would be considered a treasure of art. The length of the building is 490 feet, its breadth 298, its elevation under the dome 258. It is in the form of a Latin cross, and is supported by 52 pillars, 90 feet high and 8 feet in diameter. Its foundation was laid in 1387, by Visconti, and many distinguished artists furnished designs for its completion and embellishment.

Napoleon I, did much to hasten its completion to its present state. "In fretwork, carving and statues, it goes beyond all the churches in the world, St. Peter's itself not excepted. Its double aisles, clustered pillars, its lofty arches, the lustre of its walls, its numberless niches, all filled with marble figures, give it an appearance novel in Italy, and singularly majestic."—*Eustace.*

There is a subterranean chapel or vault beneath, where St. Charles Borromeo, clothed in his pontifical robes, studded with the most precious gems, lies buried in a magnificent sarcophagus of crystal, resting on solid silver supports, with the armorial bearings, in solid gold, of Philip IV, King of Spain, who had great veneration for the saint. The entire vault is lined with solid silver bas-reliefs, representing the most striking events in the life of this great servant of God.

There is no saint in the calendar more deeply held in reverence by the inhabitants of any city, than St. Charles, by the Milanese. And well, indeed, might they reverence him; for although made Cardinal Archbishop of Milan by his uncle, Pope Pius IV, at the extremely young age of twenty-three, never was there one more worthy of the title or the position. He was even at that age the model of every virtue, of wonderful austerity of life, purity of manner, apostolic zeal, disinterestedness and self-sacrifice. Several times did he risk his precious life whilst attending to the spiritual and corporal wants of those afflicted by the terrible plague that devastated the city of Milan in 1575; and at another time, when there was great danger of a famine, he sold one of his principalities (for he was the heir of a princely family), and distributed in one day the whole sum thus obtained (40,000 crowns) in charity to the poor. "During the continuance of the plague, which carried off some thousands of the people, he preached every day, distributed medicine and relief to the sick and poor, administered the last sacraments to the dying, and assisted in burying the dead. Three several times he walked barefoot through the city, wearing his purple robes as cardinal, and with a halter around his neck. Then kneeling before the crucifix in the cathedral, he solemnly offered himself as a sacrifice for the people. Twenty-eight priests voluntarily joined him in his ministry, and it is recorded that neither himself nor any of these caught the infection."—*Mrs. Jameson's Legends.*

After the Duomo, the next object of greatest interest in Milan, is the famous painting of the "Last Supper," by Leonardo da Vinci, which, though disfigured by time and abuse, still, to the delight of every lover of art, adorns the refectory of the old monastery formerly attached to the venerable church of Santa Maria delle Grazie. It is, indeed, a study for generations of artists, who can never hope to rival the wondrous truthfulness and variety of expression that are depicted on the countenances of our Saviour and the Apostolic Band.

It is related of Da Vinci, that after having

painted the face of St. John the Beloved Disciple, so heavenly and divine was the expression, that he was almost in despair of ever being able to render that of our Lord more remarkable for the unveiling of the divinity, which should naturally shine forth from Him. It is also said that the artist was nearly two years studying how to depict in a human countenance, the malice, treachery and depravity of Judas, until, at last, he succeeded by taking one of his bitter enemies for his desired model.

Here, in this now deserted monastery, you will see every day artists from different countries striving to imitate this incomparable *chef-d'œuvre*, thus rendering perpetual homage to the genius of that great master, the humble Da Vinci.

Leaving the beautiful city of Milan, and before entering into Switzerland, I spent a few days in Turin, a really beautifully situated and elegantly constructed city. Resting there over Sunday, I visited many of the churches, which I was delighted to find well filled from the earliest hours with crowds of respectable worshippers. The public avenues and promenades are amongst the finest in the world, and give an appearance of elegance and refinement unsurpassed by any city in Europe.

Leaving the sunny clime of Italy, I crossed the borders into

SWITZERLAND,

the land of William Tell. There is scarcely a region one may visit, which seems so mentally bracing and invigorating as this once glorious country. There is such towering majesty in its mountains, so much beauty in its lovely lakes, so much vigor, health and strength in its pure, clear, invigorating atmosphere, and such a spirit of liberty pervading its very air, that it is really mournful to think of the sad change which has come over that land, like a dark and deepening cloud, perverting it from a land of liberty, to one of persecution.

This was the sad feeling that was uppermost in

my soul, during the few days that I spent in Geneva, that grave, yet lovely situated city on the banks of the beauteous Lake Leman, with the grand, majestic old king of the mountains— Mount Blanc, with its silver-tipped crown of dazzling snow piercing the very heavens,

"In the wild pomp of mountain majesty."

Persecution rages there against the ministers of the true faith, and the saintly Bishop of Geneva, Mgr. Mermillod, is not permitted to exercise his holy functions in his own diocese, but remains banished from his country. The shades of Calvin seem to have settled once more over that entire region, and with his spirit has returned the spirit of bitter persecution.

Switzerland is indeed a lovely country for tourists, and many a scene of grandeur and of beauty is laid open to their enchanted gaze. What grand and sublime views are unfolded to sight—especially before entering, and after emerging from that most stupendous work of the age,

Mount Cenis tunnel—the unrivalled mountains, charming valleys, impetuous streams, and romantic hamlets, nestling along the mountain base, suggest everything that is lovely and soul inspiring in natural scenery.

Entering the old town of Lausanne, which is elevated above the lake, and affords a magnificent view of the surrounding country, especially from where the old cathedral stands, I visited that grand gothic edifice, which was dedicated by Pope Gregory XII, in presence of Rudolph of Hapsburgh.

Its interior is indeed very desolate, everything bare and gloomy, and there was no mark of Christian art to decorate its walls. It was evident that the spirit of Calvin, and so-called reformers, such as he, had left sad traces of occupancy by the absence of everything that is beautiful, consoling and instructive to the true Christian beholder.

Passing through Basle, the next place I stopped at was the famous old town of Mayence, where a distinguished Catholic congress was held a few weeks before. Here lived the great St. Boniface, some eleven hundred and twenty years ago, and here, also; was Guttenburg, the inventor of printing, born; in one of the fine public squares there is a statue erected to his memory. The cathedral is a remarkable old edifice, and was undergoing extensive repairs at the time I visited it.

Taking steamer at Mayence, I sailed along the glorious old

RHINE,

justly of world-wide fame for the beauty and marvellous variety of its scenery; offering perpetually new and charming pictures to the eyes; recalling the romance and history of days long gone by; the ruins of many a lordly castle, many a grand old palace and loftily situated monastery of yore, which ruins add an indescribable charm to those incomparable beauties so lavishly bestowed by the hands of bounteous nature.

Leaving Mayence, we pass the summer residence of the Duke of Nassau, at Biebrich; the famous Rheingau, with its cluster of villages, said to be the most productive and beautiful part of Germany. Here at the picturesque town of Eltville we perceive the ruins of the old Castle of Baudoin, Archbishop of Trèves in 1330; the venerable Chateau of Johannisberg, situated on an eminence three hundred and fifty feet high, entirely covered with vines; the noble heights of Niederwald, and "fair Bingen on the Rhine." Then Ingelheim, where Charlemagne was born, according to some historians, and where he built a grand palace, no trace of which now remains. You next behold the Maüsthurn (the mouse-tower of which Southey wrote), built in the thirteenth century by Archbishop Siegfried as a toll-house, now used as a signal-station; and the Castle of Ehrenfels, formerly belonging to the Archbishops of Mayence. It is evident from these and other similar well-fortified castles, such as Rheinstein and Stolzenfels, that the bishops of old were men of immense power and influence in Church and State.

Passing Ehrenbreehstein, one of the most strongly fortified Prussian strongholds, and Bonn, the seat of a University, we arrive at

COLOGNE,

more especially distinguished on account of its cathedral, which, when completed, will be the finest gothic structure in the world. The corner stone was laid in the year 1248, the choir was consecrated in 1322, and nothing more was done to complete this magnificently designed building until the beginning of this century. The interior, such as it is now, was only completed twelve years ago. The extreme length is 511 feet, and width 231. In the choir are colossal statues of our Saviour, the blessed Virgin and the twelve Apostles, and the windows are of most beautifully stained glass of the fourteenth century.

Here repose the remains of the Magi, the three kings from the East, who adored the Infant Saviour in the manger at Bethlehem. This holy shrine attracted for ages thousands of pilgrims from all parts of the world, so that Cologne became known as the "City of the Three Kings."

I was informed that there were five hundred men still at work on this grand cathedral, more especially in striving to complete the two towers, which are to be elevated to the height of five hundred feet.

In the Church of St. Gereon are buried the remains of the six thousand martyrs of the Theban Legion, who suffered for the faith under Diocletian, A.D. 286. The Church of St. Ursula is sacred to the memory of the eleven thousand virgins (supposed to have come from England), who were making a pilgrimage to Rome, and who were put to death here by the barbarous Huns.

Leaving the famous old city of Cologne, I took the cars for

Aix-la-Chapelle,

which I reached just in time to witness its grand septennial celebration on the occasion of the solemn Exposition of its grand relics. Thousands of pious pilgrims from different parts of Europe, more especially from Germany, Switzerland and Belgium, came to venerate these most precious relics, which are preserved in the old cathedral.

During an entire fortninght, that is, from the 10th to the 24th of July, what are called the "*grandes reliques*" are exposed to the veneration of the people. As this occurs only once in every seven years, we can well imagine what an immense concourse of the faithful are attracted to this venerable shrine. It was estimated that during the days of the Exposition in 1860, at least 500,000 persons visited the city, for the purpose of satisfying their devotion. Every train that enters the city brings a very large number of pious pilgrims, who throng all the streets leading to the venerable cathedral. Those visiting the shrine have all the privileges and indulgences of a jubilee accorded them, provided, of course, that they fulfill the usual conditions.

This septennial celebration dates from the 10th century, and the opening or unsealing, as well as the closing and resealing, of the relics is always attended with the most solemn ceremonies, in presence of the ecclesiastical authorities and the magistrates of the town.

Aix-la-Chapelle was always the favorite city of Charlemagne. It is generally believed that he was born here, and here likewise he was buried. He built a splendid chapel here in honor of our Blessed Lady, in the year 796, and it excited universal admiration. Having been remarkable for his piety and Christian disposition, he eagerly sought to enrich this chapel with the most precious relics, and these he received from Pope Adrian I, Leo III, and the patriarchs of Jerusalem and Constantinople.

This church has an inestimable treasure of relics which, though very precious, are called "the small relics," simply by way of distinction, and these, one is permitted to see at any time. The "great relics" are four in number:

I. The long white robe worn by the Blessed Virgin on the night of our Lord's nativity.

II. The swaddling-clothes of the infant Jesus.

III. The cloth on which the body of St. John the Baptist was laid after he had been beheaded.

IV. The linen scarf that encircled the limbs of our Saviour when he died on the cross.

These great relics were exposed every day in this fortnight to the veneration of the faithful, from ten o'clock until twelve, from the windows of the upper story of the old tower of the cathedral, amid the booming of cannon, the chanting of many voices, and the music of a brass band playing appropriate sacred airs. The windows of all the neighboring houses were previously engaged, and awnings were erected on the roofs for the accommodation of anxious spectators. But all could see and hear distinctly, even those who were assembled in the various streets leading to the church. I had, however, by kind permission, a closer view of the sacred relics, and found them in a remarkable state of preservation. There are, besides those relics I have mentioned, in costly reliquaries, enriched with most precious stones, a linen cincture, worn by the Blessed Virgin in her youth, the leathern girdle of our Saviour, one of the cords with which he was bound, a piece of the sponge and of the sacred cross, the point of one of the nails, the bones of Zachary, the father of St. John the Baptist, two teeth of St. Thomas the Apostle, and a number of other holy treasures.

After leaving Aix, we enter the dominion of

BELGIUM,

a fine, level, healthy and fertile country, and worthy of the name "garden of Europe," as it is not unappropriately called. It is a small kingdom, but no part of it is permitted to grow waste or desolate, being better cultivated and having more population to the square mile (about four hundred and thirty) than any other nation in Europe.

BRUSSELS

is a beautiful, modernized city, with fine avenues, promenades, elegant mansions and public buildings. The Cathedral, a large and noble edifice, dedicated to St. Gudule, grand-daughter of King Pepin, was begun in the year 1226, by Henry I, then Duke of Brabant, and was not finished until the 15th century. What struck me as being most worthy of notice was the grand pulpit, the work of Verbruggen, in 1699, representing the "expulsion from Paradise," the most elegant and most artistically carved pulpit perhaps in the whole world.

In one of the public squares there is a fine monument to the memory of Count Frederick de Merode (1830), of the same immediate family as the late Mgr. de Merode, who was at one time an officer in the French army in Algiers, before he became an ecclesiastic.

But as fine and well built a city as Brussels undoubtedly is, it is not by any means so interesting to visit as

GHENT,

the chief city of East Flanders, a very ancient and important town. The cathedral of St. Bavon is a grand, splendid old structure, the crypt of which dates from the tenth century, the nave and choir from the thirteenth, and the tower from the sixteenth century. The brothers Van Eyck, the first painters in oil, who executed the beautiful painting of "The Lamb," were born in this town, and buried in the cathedral crypt. There are twenty-four chapels in this magnificent edifice, each of which is inclosed with massive brass gates of most artistic workmanship. The pulpit here, as in Brussels, was the work of the famous Verbruggen, and is unsurpassed for beauty of design and exquisite finish. Here, in this grand old cathedral, I had the great pleasure of being present at a solemn *Te Deum,* in company with the esteemed and learned Canon Vandenhende, formerly president of the Theological Seminary at Troy, N. Y. The venerable bishop of the diocese intoned the *Te Deum*, which was well rendered by the choir, in honor of their annual civic festivity, and the entire garrison of the city were present, headed by their fine-looking officers, who occupied position within the choir. Although the demeanor of many of them was respectful, it was by no means difficult to perceive that no small number seemed to be affected or tainted by the so-called liberalism of the day, which, as far as I was able to learn, was doing no small injury amongst a numerous class in Belgium at the present time.

Ghent is a remarkably clean, industrious and quaint old town. Whilst passing through its orderly streets at noon, when the working classes go to dinner, or at evening, when they are returning to their humble homes, you will see thousands of thrifty workingmen and women issuing from the numerous factories, making a strange clatter on the streets and sidewalks with their wooden shoes, which seem to be almost invariably worn by the working classes in that part of the country. I was told that these wooden shoes were not at all injurious, but, on the contrary, quite conducive to the health of the operatives in factories.

Before leaving Belgium, I saw another grand and very imposing cathedral, in the beautifully located city of Antwerp. It is 500 feet in length by 250 in width, with its grand and lofty tower, 400 feet in height. It is remarkable for the possession of the masterpieces of Rubens, more especially the "Descent from the Cross," perhaps his *chef-d'œuvre*. The magnificent church of St. Jacques, where the great painter Rubens lies buried, is still more remarkable for the beauty and splendor of its decorations.

Belgium, on the whole, is a charming country, and there are many objects of decided interest in art and architecture to amply repay whatever time one may spend in visiting it.

Leaving Antwerp, I took steamer for Harwich, England, at four o'clock in the evening; and after a long and not very agreeable passage, with miserable accommodations, I arrived there next morning, and went thence by rail, 70 miles, to

LONDON.

It is truly the Babylon of modern times, with its immense population, its fearful din of traffic, its noise, its bustle and world-wide commerce. Here we find the extremes of splendor and wretchedness fully depicted in its grand avenues and squalid lanes, its lofty palaces and wretched tenements, its magnificent public buildings and "rotten rows." It is the greatest city for business and bustle in the world, and might be called, without much exaggeration, a world in itself. The public parks are numerous, spacious, sometimes beautiful, and generally well cared. Hyde Park is the finest and largest, and the principal resort of the aristocratic element at special hours.

The Prince Albert Memorial is really a superb Gothic monument, adorned with a very large number of elegant sculptures in bas-reliefs, representing the foremost names in the various branches of art, music and literature. It is estimated to have cost over a half a million of dollars, and is not yet completed.

The greatest object of interest in London is the grand old

"WESTMINISTER ABBEY,"

which recalls the memories of the grandest days of the monastic past, when England was truly Catholic, and its kings and princes vied with each other in building, adorning and endowing such noble and useful structures, where perpetual praises were sung to the Almighty, and whence the light of science diffused itself over the nation.

Here lie buried kings and queens from the time of Edward the Confessor (whose tomb is still here under the high altar), statesmen, warriors, poets, orators, philosophers, historians and philanthropists.

Passing by the hundreds of tombs and memorial tablets, how many ages of history are recalled to one's mind; how varied the characters of the illustrious personages buried here, and how many, whose remains are here side by side, who were fierce and bitter enemies in life. Here lie the ashes of the vain and cruel Queen Elizabeth, and there all that is mortal of the noble but unfortunate Mary, Queen of Scots, whom she fiercely persecuted unto death. There the Edwards and the Henrys, kings of England, and that soul of mediæval chivalry, Richard Cœur de Leon; then the great poets, orators, statesmen—Chaucer, Spencer, Johnson, Gay, Dryden, Sheridan, Pitt, Chatham, Canning and Palmerston, and hosts of others who occupy lofty niches in the temple of fame.

Before leaving London, I had the pleasure and the honor of an interview with that great and zealous prelate, Archbishop, now

CARDINAL MANNING,

the glory of the Catholic Church in England. He is a man of striking appearance that never fails to impress and interest. He is somewhat of that type of countenance which we might call of mediæval character; of rather sharp features; deep, penetrating, expressive eyes; pale, attenuated, mortified-looking face, full of mental vigor, ardent zeal and active faith; and his *tout ensemble* would impress you as a prelate deeply in earnest with the great work of conversion of a great nation. His manner of conversation is remarkable for clearness, logical precision and quiet yet ardent zeal.

Leaving all the noise and bustle of this modern Babylon behind me, I took the afternoon train for Holyhead, where I arrived in time to take the mail steamer for Dublin, via Kingstown, and there I arrived one Sunday morning, in August.

Though

IRELAND

was the last country I visited, it was by no means the last in my affections. As I approached the Irish coast and got a glimpse of the dear old isle, with its magnificent verdure, my heart throbbed with no common emotion, and various were the feelings that struggled for the ascendency.

There it stood before me, in all its reality, that emerald isle of the ocean, which I had so long desired to behold; there it stood enshrined in all the beauty and loveliness that a most bounteous nature could bestow; that land of heroes and of saints, warriors and poets, orators, wits and scholars; the land of St. Patrick, St. Bridget and St. Columbkille; of Sarsfield, Emmet, Curran and Grattan, Father Mathew and O'Connell; and of innumerable martyrs for country and for faith. Surely when I put my foot on its shores, I felt that every sod of it was sacred and consecrated by the blood of countless martyrs for God and their native land.

> "Lives there a man with soul so dead,
> That never to himself hath said,
> This is my own, my native land."

Dublin

is a fine, orderly, well-built city, certainly one of the most beautifully situated capitals in the world, and surrounded with lovely and enchanting scenery. There is an air of comfort and respectability about it that richer cities possess not, so that Ireland may well be proud of its chief city, which can bear a favorable comparison with some of the first in other parts of Europe. It has many fine, grand old structures, such as the former Parliament building, now the Bank of Ireland, the famous Trinity College and the Four Courts—a solemn, grave and imposing edifice. Then the inhabitants of Dublin may well pride themselves on their grand and extensive Phœnix Park, which can favorably compare with any in the world, and is certainly not equalled by any public park in England. The air is bracing and invigorating, and the surrounding scenery adds immensely to the charm, to say nothing of the exhilaration which is produced by enjoying the magnificent views on every side whilst riding on the famous Irish "jaunting car," which is warranted to keep one's eyes open to every beauty of scenery by its gay, lively, rollicking style, and the witty, enjoyable comments of those pleasant, yet good-natured drivers to be found only in the Green Isle.

In no part of the world have I seen the Sunday more strictly or more religiously observed than in this noble old capital. Here (and in fact it is the same throughout Ireland, in the principal towns and cities), it is easy to observe the deep and solid piety of the Irish people. Not as in many other parts of Europe, is piety confined to the female portion of the community, which fact is clearly proved by the large number of men and women, from different ranks in society, who attend the masses at the various hours on week days, and the proportionately large number that approach the sacred table on all feasts of any particular note in the calendar.

They have a learned, zealous and estimable clergy, presided over by an able episcopate, at the head of which is the learned yet modest and unassuming Cardinal Archbishop of Dublin, who is so kindly, gracious and courteous in his manner.

Before leaving Dublin I did not fail to visit

GLASNEVIN CEMETERY,

which is beautifully laid out, and gives evidence of care and attention. Here repose the remains of Grattan, and here also the body of the Immortal Liberator—Daniel O'Connell—Ireland's proudest boast. The monument erected over the splendid vault is a very lofty structure, representing by its form one of the ancient round towers of Ireland, thus symbolizing the glories of its past history, the triumphs of the present century through the great Emancipator, and the hopes of the future, when Ireland shall once more take its stand among the leading nations of the earth.

I entered the vault, and, with reverence, placed my hand on the coffin which contains whatever remains of the mighty form of the uncrowned king of the isle of saints and scholars. I visited the county (Kerry) where he was born, passed by the lovely city (Genoa) where he breathed his last, saw, with emotion, where his noble heart was entombed in the venerable church of St. Agatha, attached to the Irish College in Rome, and now stood by the grand mausoleum where the giant intellect reposes in the silence of the tomb.

Passing on to

Cork,

the capital of the south of Ireland, I found it to be a nicely situated city, with fine quays and wide avenues, and a people extremely generous and hospitable. It is certainly a place where one may spend many pleasant days. Patrick street is a handsome thoroughfare, and is adorned with a life-like figure of the great apostle of temperance, Father Mathew, which was erected by the citizens when the late lamented John Francis Maguire was Mayor of Cork.

The lovers of the romantic may stroll with pleasure through the lovely Mardyke, one of the handsomest promenades in the whole of Europe, and gently resounding on their ears come the sounds from afar, of

>—the bells of Shandon,
> That sound so grand on
>   The pleasant waters of the River Lee;

and then memories of "Father Prout" arise over the fair city, and lend an affectionate charm to the beauty of the scenery.

Whilst spending some time in Cork, I received some intelligence from home with regard to an article that appeared in one of our county papers, from a certain reverend gentleman who happened to be "doing Europe," as it is termed, about the same time that I myself was on my tour. It seems to me that he was "doing" it very quickly, and, moreover, *not doing* justice to the Irish people on the question of education.

The reverend gentleman stated that he only saw *one school-house* on the road from Cork to Killarney, and that the priests are, as usual, keeping the people in ignorance. Now, it is not at all unlikely that the reverend gentleman saw only one building that looked like a school-house, whilst he was comfortably seated in an express car, flying at the rate of about forty miles an hour between Cork and Killarney; but had he taken time to stop on the way, and, laying aside his very bitter prejudices, carefully inquire and examine, he would have been astonished at the great number of schools in proportion to the population, and the excellent manner in which they were managed.

Of course they do not build their school-houses in that country directly on the line of railroad, so that our American tourists may see and note them as they pass by, comfortably seated "first-class" in express trains; but they build them in the villages, sometimes a few miles distant from the railroad depots, where the pupils and their parents reside.

Now, on hearing the above charge, I made it my duty to inquire and personally examine, and I found out to my satisfaction that there was not a single parish in the district of country referred to, that was not amply supplied with schools, some having as many as four, six, eight and ten, and all under the supervision of the faithful clergy. It would be difficult to find in any county a district so well attended to in matters of education as the one to which reference is made, and many of the schools are admirably controlled and directed, especially those under the care of the Presentation monks and nuns.

Before leaving Cork, I, of course, paid a visit to the famous "Blarney Castle,"-but as to the famous "Blarney Stone" itself, which Father Prout says:

> "That whoever kisses
> Oh! he never misses
> To grow eloquent,"

I must say, I did not venture to "osculate," for fear I should ever be accused of indulging in that sort of persuasive elequence so peculiar to those who have sought their inspiration from such a source. There may have been another reason too, in the fact of its being so difficult to reach, as you have to be "hung by the heels" in order to impress your lips on the sacred stone.

But of all the delightful places a person may visit, there is not one that can compare with the

LAKES OF KILLARNEY,

and the surrounding scenery, in which they are set as in a beautiful framework of richest gems. These lakes, with their mountain guardians, combine everything that is calm and grand, peaceful and towering, lovely, charming, varied and picturesque. Nature seems to have formed here her masterpiece of beauty and loveliness. Here she has expended most bounteously all her wonderful wealth, in crag and mountain peak, shady nooks, romantic isles, fantastically-shaped rocks and verdure wonderful to behold. And added to these striking peculiarities, as well as beauties of scenery, the various strange legends and romantic tales clinging to every rock, and isle, and lofty peak, giving a fresh charm and new pleasure to every part of the scenery, as it unfolds itself before our enraptured gaze.

Then the merry laugh, the smiling face, the sparkling wit, the strange tales and droll songs of the boatmen add no small variety to the charm, and leave on the memory of the voyager from distant shores remembrance of happy scenes that cannot soon be effaced.

Many a pleasant and most enjoyable day may be spent in this lovely locality. The lovers of the romantic cannot fail to find much to admire amid the wild grandeur of the Gap of Dunloe, and the constantly varying scenes of the three lakes, with their pretty inlets, picturesque bays, charming islands, rich shrubbery, quaint rocks and stern-looking old mountains jealously keeping guard over the precious treasures of beauty lying peacefully at their feet. Here are to be seen the grand Torc Cascade and the O'Sullivan Cascade with its triple waterfall; the "Eagle's Nest," a rocky ascent of seven hundred feet; Mangerton and Purple Mountains; Arbutus Island with its luxuriant growth of bush and tree, and "Sweet Innisfallen," the once beautiful retreat of the Monks of old, about which Moore sang in such poetic strains:

> "Sweet Innisfallen, fare thee well;
> May calm and sunshine long be thine;
> How fair thou art let others tell,
> While but to feel how fair be mine.

> "Sweet Innisfallen, long shall dwell
> In memory's dream that sunny smile
> Which o'er thee on that evening fell,
> When first I saw thy fairy isle."

Then, who would fail to visit Muckrose Abbey, one of the loveliest of ruins, round which kind nature has entwined the very tendrils of its heart in ivy green, imparting new life and beauty, though its walls now are silent and no longer resound to the midnight chant in praise of God.

Within these hallowed precincts are the tombs of those venerated chiefs of old: The O'Sullivan Beare, the O'Donoghoe and McCarthy More.

Irishmen may well be proud of their country, for with all the misery of its past history, it has charms which no land can surpass, beauties which its tyrants could never efface, and glories that shall last as long as Christianity itself. Ireland is noble, beautiful and grand even in its ruins— ruins which tell of its former glorious history, its sacred chapels and monasteries, and famous schools of old, that spread its reputation throughout Europe in the ages when other nations were almost entirely plunged in barbarism. It may well be called "the gem of the sea," on account of its most smiling verdure, its wonderful fertility, the beauty of its lakes, the grandeur of its mountains, its noble rivers, its picturesque and romantic scenery.

It is still more lovely and interesting on account of its grand old history, its long ages of fiercest persecution, its invincible faith and undaunted Christian heroism. Worthy of all admiration, in fine, is it likewise for the noble characteristics of its impoverished people, their generosity of heart, nobility of spirit, cheerfulness even in the direst adversity, and tender devotion to all that is noble, holy or sacred in nature or religion.

Before leaving Ireland, I visited the quaint old town of Dingle (picturesquely located on the western coast of Kerry), the cradle of my ancestors, and the venerable old house where my eyes first opened on the world, although my recollections of the place were indeed of the faintest and most indistinct character. Near this old town is St. Brendan's Hill, and two or three miles distant, Ventry Harbor, where a famous battle was fought. Journeying on to Queenstown (formerly the Cove of Cork), one of the finest harbors in the world, I took steamer for New York.

Much, indeed, as I enjoyed my visit to other lands, and appreciated the mildness of other climes; much as I admired their varied beauties, the grandeur of their temples, the glory of their ancient monuments, and felt the enchantment naturally produced by rambling amid historic ruins, it was with no small feelings of joy, gladness and satisfaction that I put foot once more in our own free

AMERICA,

which we love and esteem all the more, the longer we are absent, and the farther we travel away from it. This, I believe, is the feeling of all who were either born or reared and educated in this great republic; for here we have a country of which we may well be proud, and which gives us no cause to sigh for other climes. Here there is no lack of beauty in nature, of lovely, grand and picturesque scenery, magnificent chains of mountains, lakes of wonderful extent, rivers of great length and majestic flow, and a soil teeming with wealth and productiveness.

The Rhine is indeed a most beautiful river, but it is not so majestic as our noble Hudson, which combines all that is beautiful, grand and picturesque in scenery, giving us something of the wild grandeur of the Giant's Causeway of Ireland, in our Palisades, with much of the loveliness of scenery of Lake Como in Italy, and not a little of the picturesque character of the Rhine. All it lacks is the romance of history to deck its lofty hill-tops and beautiful slopes with ruins of castles, towers and "monasteries grave."

Moreover, Europe has nothing to compare with Niagara Falls, which, for real grandeur and sublimity, stands unrivalled in the world; and in fact there are not many scenes of beauty in other lands which will not be found equalled, if not surpassed, in some part of our well-nigh boundless country. Adding to all this the very freedom of the air we breathe, where every man feels that he is a man, with corresponding rights and duties, then we have every reason to thank God for the manifold blessings we possess, and never prove recreant to our trusts.

www.ingramcontent.com/pod-product-compliance
Lightning Source LLC
Chambersburg PA
CBHW020147170426
43199CB00010B/918